TRANSFORM DIFFICULTIES INTO TRIUMPHS IN 30 DAYS

A Story-Based Workbook to Guide You to Turn Difficulties into Triumphs by Carol Knox

"The capacity to turn tragedy into triumph is a logotherapy theme that Carol Knox has picked up throughout her self-help workbook. She challenges the reader to do it in 30 days and hence the book itself is arranged around 30 day by day stories, action plans and personal reflections.

From the organization of chapters there seems to be an assumption that the book will be picked up by someone at the bottom of their trough in life, the first chapter, This too shall pass, implies as much as does the second, Finding something to live for is critical. Knox then moves the reader through searching for meaning in life and particularly a focus on finding meaning from suffering. As the reader learns to be compassionate with the self and to appreciate the life they have, the turning point in therapeutic terms seems to be intended on day 13 Your watershed moment.

However, Knox also suggests that it is possible to select any particular story simply for its inspirational message. Hence the person feeling on top of their game right now might choose to begin at Day 26 Igniting humour…

…This could be a powerful 30 day journey, or more like 30 weeks, that could change a life. It is most likely to be used by dipping into one or a few of the stories rather than the more demanding 30 day journey. It is a book that all logotherapists might consider putting in their reference library of client resources."
- Paul McQuillan PHD, Director at <u>LifeChange Therapies</u>, Brisbane, Australia.

"Carol Knox's story-based workbook is a true gem with highly relatable and relevant stories about human triumphs in the face

of adversity and pain. The workbook provides helpful cues for reflection and highlights specific aspects of healing stories that connect to your own life experience. What's more, the workbook prompts you to come up with your personal actions to put your reflections into practice in your life, thus making your insights immediately – and meaningfully - actionable. Frankl's concepts really come to life – in your life – transforming suffering, pain and difficulties into uniquely human triumphs. Your triumphs!"
- Sabine Indinger Logotherapy Practitioner and Logotherapy@Work Coach, Austria

"I love your book! I have read it a couple of times and I think it is a rich source of inspiration, wise words and practical suggestions. I would buy it for myself and give it as a gift. I think it will lead to 'ah ha' moments and could be life changing for some people."
- Carol Barton, Positive Psychology Coach, United Kingdom

"Human potential at its best is to transform a tragedy into a personal triumph, to turn one's predicament into a human achievement."

— **Viktor Frankl,** *Man's Search for Meaning.*

Dedication

I dedicate this workbook to all those who have touched my life and coloured the world to become a better place.

Preface

Introduction

A lack of meaning might be called a malaise of our times.

When we encounter challenges or difficulties in life, often

we discover that we can't find a centre, a way to cope.

What is it all about?

About

This workbook offers daily ways for you to overcome

difficult situations, to help you to find the WHY that will

energise and animate your life. In finding your own WHY,

in discovering your meaning and your purpose, your pain

will be lessened. You will discover ways to unfold

meaning, as well as a personal calling, through tasks that

you can fulfil, relationships that you can strengthen and

enrich, and attitudes that you can develop and cultivate.

The workbook can be used flexibly, daily, weekly or by selecting days that resonate with you.

This practical, inspiring, and potentially life-changing workbook will take you step by step through a process towards a more fulfilled and enriched working and personal life.

Overview of Stories

In this story-based workbook, stories are offered to guide you to discover and unfold your unique meaning and purpose in life, even during difficult times.

It includes **personal stories**, as well as **stories about others** such as Viktor Frankl, Nelson Mandela, Beethoven, Helen Keller, Jack Kerouac, James Hillman, Helen Martins, The Buddha, Temple Grandin, Tara Brach, Carl Rogers, a Taoist story, an Indian fable, Henry Ford,

Thomas Edison, Albert Einstein, a story from Logotherapy and Jerry Long.

Acknowledgements

My motivation for creating this workbook grew out of my need to make available to as wide a group of people as possible the potential to overcome life difficulties and transform these into triumphs. Initially many of these stories were to form part of a PHD research project with trauma sufferers. Due to ill health, I was unable to continue with this research. I began to think about how I could use this material in a different way, so that it could reach more people and potentially enrich their lives. In this way, the workbook came into being. My life purpose is to help others to discover and unfold their purpose and unique meaning and calling in life.

I am deeply grateful to my daughter Kana, who has been unwavering in her support of all the projects I have undertaken and in all the life changes I have experienced over the years.

My thanks go to my editor Liz Dexter from Libroediting.com. Liz completed the editing quickly and was very helpful in her comments and in discovering accurate references.

My thanks also go to my beta reader David Owens.

Table of Days

"Human potential at its best is to transform a tragedy into a personal triumph, to turn one's predicament into a human achievement."

— **Viktor Frankl,** *Man's Search for Meaning.*

§

Day 1 – This Too Shall Pass

Story (Personal Story): Standing amongst boxes, piles of clothes, curious cats, distressed dogs, confused and angry children, I looked around at what was left of my married life. The empty room echoed as I absorbed the end of a relationship, the end of a home and the chaos around me. I sank to the floor, overwhelmed by the pain, my face wet with tears. I thought in that moment of the saying, *"this too shall pass"*. I thought of Viktor Frankl, a holocaust survivor, who speaks of *"freedom of the will"*. The significance for me was to really take into my being this freedom, this knowledge that as difficult as these moments were, they would pass, realising I was free to choose my attitude. I decided right then to name the emotion, pain, feeling it in my heart: it felt like a hand squeezing my heart. Picturing the emotion of pain as a cloud overhead, I saw it passing away, as if blown by the wind. I continued to do this until the emotion lost its power, passed away with my naming and acceptance of it, by my choice to let it pass.

Story Essence: No matter how difficult a situation is, know it will pass. Everything changes. Really knowing that something painful will pass, deep in the very pores of your being, embracing this and taking it to heart, can profoundly change the way you experience difficult situations. Our ability to choose our response is our freedom. Despite limitations, how do we transcend the constraints imposed by our environments?

Specific Action: Consider your painful experiences. Keep a journal and write about how you feel over the next week. When you feel a strong emotion, name the emotion, whether it's loneliness, embarrassment or pain. The purpose of naming your emotion is to get a clear idea of what the emotion is, because it can be hard to describe.

Once you know what it is exactly, you can work to lessen it. Also, you can begin to recognise the feeling of it in your body. Now visualise the emotion as an overhead cloud, which inevitably will float away. The anguish you feel will lessen and eventually pass away.

By naming the emotion of pain, feeling it in your body, and visualising it as a cloud that passes away, you can lessen the distress of a difficult experience. Tomorrow, we will consider the benefits of finding something to live for.

Day 1 – My Notes

17

§

Day 2 – Finding Something to Live for is Critical

Story (Nelson Mandela): Nelson Mandela was convicted of conspiracy to overthrow the State of South Africa and sentenced to life in prison. Living in a tiny cell on the inhospitable Robben Island, with a bucket for a toilet, he toiled long hours in a blazing hot quarry by day. He was allowed one visitor a year, and for only thirty minutes. This experience transformed him as he kept his focus on bearing his situation with dignity, using his charm and intelligence to become a leader of his comrades in prison. After 27 years in prison, he emerged from these trials to lead South Africa to democracy. Many call him the Father of the Nation – Madiba or Tata. He kept his mind active, studying law at night. In focusing on leading others, he found something to live for: he stayed hopeful.

Nietzsche said: *"He who has a why to live for can bear*

almost any how".[1] When I have travelled in the past and people ask me where I am from, when I say South Africa, they always ask about Madiba. The last time was when he was ill in hospital. In an airport, I stopped a cleaner to ask where the public phones were. He asked me: "How is Madiba, we hear he is sick?"

Story Essence: We can see in the story of Nelson Mandela that, if we have a why to live for, we can go through almost any circumstance that doesn't kill us. Madiba is an example to all of us that no matter how hard things are, we can always find ways to create meaning and hope. It is clear that we all yearn for something to live for, to give meaning to our lives. It is this ineffable

---

[1] "He [who] knows the 'why' for his existence ... will be able to bear almost any 'how'". Viktor Frankl (1905–1997), in *Man's Search for Meaning* (1946), was likely quoting Friedrich Nietzsche (1844–1900) from his *Twilight of the Idols, or How to Philosophize with a Hammer* (1889): "If we have our own why in life, we shall get along with almost any how". Or: "If we have our own why in life, we shall get along with almost any how." *Twilight of the Idols, Maxims & Arrows*, #12. Variant translation: "He who has a why to live for can bear almost any how".

'something', our yearning for meaning, our yearning to find a why, that motivates us, that energises and animates our lives.

Specific Action: Think about your own 'why'. What is it that makes your own life worth living right now? Write down your thoughts.

When you find it, you'll realise that the yearning created by a need to fulfil that purpose will far outweigh the pain that you're going through. Tomorrow we will consider the meaning we can find from life.

Day 2 – My Notes

§

Day 3 – The Question of Meaning in Life

Story (Viktor Frankl, Man's Search for Meaning): There were those who walked upright into the gas chambers, with a prayer on their lips.

Viktor Frankl talks about how spiritual life can deepen, even in a concentration camp. He noticed that those who had a rich inner life seemed to manage better, even though they were not as physically strong as others. When battered by inescapable suffering, these people were able to retreat inside themselves and enrich their spiritual selves. The meaning of life is not a question that can be put in general terms. Frankl says this would be like asking a chess champion: *"Tell me, Master, what is the best move in the world?"* [2] There is no such thing as a best or even a good

---

[2] Viktor Frankl, *Man's Search for Meaning.*

move, other than the particular situation in a given game and the personality of one's opponent. Similarly, the meaning of a person's life is in the moment. Each person has their own unique mission to carry out, something that demands fulfilment. In this sense, no person can be replaced. As each life situation challenges us or presents us with a problem to solve, the question of the meaning of life can be reversed. We can rather ask: *"what does life expect of us?"*[3] We each need to recognise that we are being questioned by life and we can only answer for our own lives, by taking responsible action, which satisfies our conscience as the right thing to do.

Story Essence: Viktor Frankl says life questions us about our meaning, which we can only know moment by moment as we are challenged by life. We are expected to

---

[3] Viktor Frankl. In his words: "...it did not really matter what we expected from life, but rather what life expected from us." *Man's Search for Meaning.*

respond responsibly to this challenge from life. We are required to answer the call. We need to be responsible for our choices, by making choices that are right for the challenge in that moment.

Specific Action: Write down the things in your life that you find meaningful and that make you believe that life is worth living. List the most important first. Give some thought to these things. Are there any that you could give more focus to?

By asking the question: *"what does life expect of us?"* we are able to change our focus from our difficulties and worries about the problems of our lives by rather focusing on our own unique meanings that we can fulfil. Tomorrow we will look more closely at the importance of love in creating a meaningful life.

Day 3 – My Notes

25

§

Day 4 – Love Can Come to the Rescue

Story (Viktor Frankl, Man's Search for Meaning): Stumbling through darkness and over icy stones and other obstacles in the cold and the unseen, everything was hushed except for the shouting of guards, a person marching beside me whispered quietly behind his hand: *"If our wives could see us now! I do hope they are better off in their camps and don't know what is happening to us."* This created an unspoken bond between Viktor Frankl and his marching mate, who knew that each was thinking of their wife. Occasionally looking up at the sky, Viktor was still able to appreciate the pink morning peeping into the day. The image of his wife swam clear and acutely into his mind, imagining her look, her answers to his conversation. It was this look, which Viktor saw so precisely, that he called *"more luminous than the sun"*. It was through this experience that Frankl was able to say that, *"the salvation of man is in love and through love."*

Story Essence: The experience of love is essential to the quality of our lives. It is the appreciation of what is beautiful, authentic and genuine about another which gives meaning to our lives. It is through thinking lovingly of those who are beloved that we can endure even awful circumstances and still know a kind of happiness.

Specific Action: Think about your experiences of the value of what is loving, beautiful and true. How do you experience this love, beauty and truth in your life? It can be through the love of a romantic partner, a relative, a companion pet or simply a friend. Write down your thoughts about these feelings and experiences. Whenever you find yourself sinking into despair, choose instead to reflect on this beauty.

Love can come to our rescue in times of despair. Simply thinking loving thoughts can lessen the pain that you might be feeling and help you to get through the storm that may be raging right now. Tomorrow we will talk about the value of creating something that could help us to feel responsible and meaningfully part of life.

Day 4 – My Notes

29

§

Day 5 – Putting your Focus on a Project

Story (Viktor Frankl, Man's Search for Meaning): Close to tears from pain and the meanness of a life reduced to a constant concern for keeping alive, Frankl found a way to lift himself out of this abject misery. By forcing his thoughts to turn to something else away from the pain, the searing cold and petty concerns, he found somehow a way to lift himself out of his oppression. He saw himself on a lecture platform of the future, in warm and pleasant conditions, his audience focusing on his every word. In this way, the sufferings of this moment were seen as somehow already in the past. It is this future focus on the creative projects we can still achieve that allows us to unfold meaning towards which we can aim.

Story Essence: Frankl points here to the importance of projects, things we can still achieve, or creative values, in unfolding meaning in our lives. He noticed that those who lost this future orientation very quickly gave up and died. My wish for you is to find your own unique meaningful activities and projects which you can look towards in the future. In this way, you make your own future.

Specific Action: Think about projects that you can undertake. What are these projects and how can you act responsibly in creating these projects or bringing these ideas to life? What do you really enjoy doing? What are the things that you do that keep you absorbed? Write down your thoughts. Picture yourself working on these projects. Better yet, begin to work on these projects.

As you find yourself focusing on and engaging in these projects, your mind will not have the opportunity to dwell on your situation, no matter how undesirable it may be.

Tomorrow we will consider what you can do if you can't change your circumstances.

Day 5 – My Notes

33

§

Day 6 – The Power of Your Mind-Set

Story (Ludwig Van Beethoven): At the age of 26, Beethoven began to go deaf. This caused him great isolation and difficulties in personal, professional and social settings. As he suffered this tragedy, he resolved to rise above it. Even with this personal tragedy, Beethoven imagined and realised seven symphonies, several piano concertos and sonatas, an opera and numerous other chamber pieces and 'occasional' music. He is recognised as an icon of music, having redefined classical music from classicism to 19th century romanticism. His music has even represented Earth, having been deployed on two Voyager probes to outer space. Viktor Frankl says, *"The way in which a man accepts his fate and all the suffering it entails, the way in which he takes up his cross, gives him ample opportunity — even under the most difficult circumstances — to add a deeper meaning to his life".[4]*

Story Essence: It is extremely important to adjust your mind-set in circumstances that you can't control. Instead of feeling that a situation is futile, you could turn it around and begin taking a different mind-set. Begin looking for how the situation can make you better. You'll amaze yourself at how quickly you can transcend the futility purely through changing your mind-set. By changing your attitude, not only do difficult situations become more bearable; they can catapult you into a higher level of existence.

Specific Action: Think about your experiences of situations over which you have no control. Write down ways in which you can change your mind-set from helplessness to having a resolve to rise above the

---

[4] *Man's Search for Meaning.*

circumstances. Become more aware of your mind-set, and watch how the change in it alters your perception of your situation. Make notes of how you have been able to make changes to your thinking.

Our mind-set in a difficult situation can not only lift us out of the storm, but can help us to rise to a higher level of existence. We will consider the possible meaning of suffering tomorrow.

Day 6 – My Notes

37

§

Day 7 – Finding Meaning from Suffering

Story (Helen Keller): Helen Keller once said: *"All the world is full of suffering, it is also full of overcoming it"*.[5] Helen overcame the enormous adversities of deafness, blindness and muteness. She courageously fought to communicate with the outside world and in the process she created a life of accomplishment and fulfilment. Helen became a well-known celebrity and lecturer, who shared her experiences with audiences, and worked to help others living with disabilities. In choosing to help others even while suffering yourself, you find your meaning and direct your mind away from your own suffering. You overcome

---

[5] Helen Keller, What is the IWW? (1918): Speech given at the New York City Civic Club, January 1918, quoted in Helen Keller: Her Socialist Years (International Publishers, 1967).

your own suffering by helping others through their suffering.

Story Essence: Helen Keller's life teaches us that the process of finding meaning in suffering does not lie in feeling like a victim of your fate. Instead, it comes from overcoming your suffering by reaching out and helping others. Rather than being a victim, you become a victor.

Specific Action: Today, think about how you can begin helping others, even through your own pain. Yes, it might seem like you first need to get over your own hurt and anger before you can help others. But, you'll find that as you begin to help others, you'll find meaning in your own suffering, while simultaneously realising the joy that comes from helping others. Write down your ideas.

By reaching out to and helping others in their suffering, you create your own meaning, as well as taking your mind off your own problems and struggles. Tomorrow we will

look more closely at other possible meanings of suffering.

Day 7 – My Notes

41

§

Day 8 – Turn Suffering into a Challenge

Story (Viktor Frankl, Man's Search for Meaning): The guard looked at him, stripped as he was of all that identified him, his clothes, his shoes, his name and now his manuscript. The guard tore up the manuscript and called it *"rubbish!"* This manuscript contained Frankl's life's work. He had hoped to save it at any cost. The grin of the guard as he realised its significance to Frankl, a pitying, then mocking and insulting look, brought home to him with a deep chill how he was really stripped of everything. Frankl decided in that moment that his life as it had been was dead to him. But at the same time he refused to *"run into the wire"*. Frankl was trapped in a concentration camp in Nazi Germany. In those days people in the same circumstances, out of despair, would run into the electrified fencing to end their suffering. He resolved in that moment that he was up to the challenge. We have a choice to think of the suffering we experience in life as a challenge. As Frankl says: *"Suffering is intended to guard us from our apathy, from psychic rigor mortis. In fact, we mature in suffering, grow because of it – it makes us richer and stronger."*

Story Essence: Although we don't have to suffer to learn, the only way to take advantage of suffering is to work out what it's here to teach us. In the supreme difficulties of the concentration camps, Frankl rose to the challenge of his suffering by refusing to give up; he chose to grow, even through the suffering.

Specific Action: Thinking about the situation you're currently facing, and ask yourself "How can this situation make me into a better, more resilient person? How can I better rise to the challenge? How can I turn it into a victorious moment?"

When you see your difficult situations as opportunities to rise to the challenge, your perspective will change completely. Instead of shrinking away from life's challenges, you'll face them head-on. Tomorrow we will look at how fear limits us.

Day 8 – My Notes

45

§

Day 9 – Is Fear Holding You Back from Your Calling?

Story (1991 film, Defending your Life, directed by Albert Brooks): In the 1991 film, *Defending your Life*, the protagonist Dan Miller, has a defence attorney named Bob Diamond, who confronts him with his own fear. Diamond says: *"Fear is like a giant fog, it sits on your brain and blocks everything. Real feeling, true happiness, real joy can't get through that fog but you lift it and buddy, you're in for the ride of your life."* Think about this for a second. If we were to come to the end of our life story today, would our lives testify for, or against us? Would our fear have prevented us from taking stock and searching for meaning? Do we need to wait for a life crisis or problem before we take stock? None of us know when the moment of the loss of life will come. Are we going to allow the fog of our own fear prevent us from finding our calling, our purpose?

Story Essence: If life is something we can lose, what have we achieved with our lives? Did we discover our purpose, our calling? Did we break through the fog of our own fears and fulfil our reason for coming onto this Earth?

Specific Action: How has fear stopped you from creating something, experiencing new situations or relationships, or changing your attitude towards something or someone? Write down your thoughts and ideas around this. In what small way can you create something, do something new or change your attitude towards something? Choose one small step today to help you to lift the veil of fear!

If suffering calls us to account for our lives, then we need to reach out and press through the fog of our fears and take on our challenges in ways that are dignified, that are responsible. By doing this, our current problems and challenges take on new meaning, new hope. Tomorrow we will look at self-compassion.

Day 9 – My Notes

§

Day 10 – Learning Self-Compassion

Story (Personal Story): Standing amongst my boxes and the chaos of the end of my married life, one of the things I did was to blame myself. In my pain and sadness I thought: why have I failed; why have I allowed this to happen? It was my fault, surely? I was supposed to be able to fix things. I was so hard on myself and so unforgiving. This made the pain of all the loss almost unbearable. It was only over time that I came to realise that I could only be 50% responsible for the failure of my marriage, that I could not expect myself to be 100% responsible, nor could I blame myself entirely. My thoughts of, "you idiot, you are a failure!" gradually lessened, helping to reduce the intensity of the pain.

Story Essence: By realising how hard I was on myself, how I felt 100% responsible for the failure of my marriage, how I engaged in negative self-talk, berating myself in my inner dialogue, I was able to give myself the essential gift of self-compassion. Being harsh and demanding of ourselves makes life even more difficult than it already is. Instead, by freeing ourselves of the full responsibility that we often carry all too easily, we can give ourselves this essential kindness, a compassion for our own human frailty. We are just as we are. Embracing this is life-affirming.

Specific Action: Think about your own negative self-talk. What are the things that you say to yourself? How can you show compassion and kindness to yourself instead? Write down your negative self-speak, and then stop yourself when you find yourself doing it and replace these thoughts with compassion towards yourself. Think kindly of yourself. Give yourself permission to do this. Think of times you have been kind, or have received kindness. Hold this feeling, let it sink in.

By stopping your self-blame and negative self-talk and instead replacing these with acceptance and self-compassion, you can change your almost unbearable pain into something you can cope with. Over time, this grows into a life-affirming habit. Tomorrow we will look at suffering as inspiration.

Day 10 – My Notes

53

§

Day 11 – Suffering can be an Inspiration

Story (Viktor Frankl, Man's Search for Meaning): Trying to inspire other inmates held captive with him in the Nazi concentration camps during WWII, Frankl encouraged them to think of themselves as being watched. He called on them to imagine themselves as surrounded by a crowd of witnesses, who looked on at them in their times of difficulty: a friend, a spouse, someone living or dead, God, a protective being. Frankl called on them not to disappoint these deeply concerned and caring people or beings. He called on them to carry their sufferings with pride, to bear them with dignity, to take note of their attitudes as if they may be called at some future date to relate how they had borne their trials. By bearing our sufferings in an honourable way, we can achieve a deep fulfilment.

Story Essence: By bearing suffering with dignity, you can be inspired to lift yourself out of your immediate surroundings and sufferings.

Specific Action: Think about how you can lift yourself out of the situation you are suffering in right now. Imagine yourself being watched by someone you respect deeply as you go through this ordeal. Journal about how you can carry yourself with dignity in this situation. You will feel stronger and more able to cope. Smile because you can.

As you practise carrying yourself with dignity in your suffering, you will be inspired to feel differently and more positively about your situation. Tomorrow we will look at suffering as a way to appreciate life right now.

Day 11 – My Notes

§

Day 12 – Appreciating Life Right Now

Story (Personal Loss): I walked up the hill towards the guest house, crying, I felt bereft, having said goodbye to someone I love, not knowing if I would see him again. For some reason this goodbye wrenched at my gut and squeezed my heart most painfully. This painful fleeting moment was a precursor of what was to come. Years later I heard through the grapevine that this person most dear to me had committed suicide. Having lost touch and hearing about his death in this way compounded the anguish that I felt. Why should we appreciate life in the moment? Because life is right now, there is no other time; we may never have a chance to capture these moments again.

Story Essence: In recognising the reality of how temporary and fleeting life is, we can value it in all its complexity. In overcoming the fear of suffering, we wipe away our illusions and face the fact that we cannot escape pain, sorrow or death. In becoming aware of how transient life is, we can better focus on finding the treasure in every single moment. When taking on suffering as a task, we can triumph, recognising that all life is meaningful. We cannot very well wait for life to begin when the chaos and suffering is over. We must live life now, while we have the opportunity to do so!

Specific Action: Think about how you can open your eyes to your own fear of suffering. What can you do to triumph over this fear? What can you do to appreciate life right now? Resolve today that this situation cannot continue to rob you of these precious moments of life that you have on Earth.

In coming to understand life as it is, impermanent, filled with all kinds of opportunities and moments, by taking on suffering as a task, we lose our fear of it and in this way achieve a genuine triumph over it. Tomorrow we

will look at suffering as a watershed experience.

Day 12 – My Notes

§

Day 13 – Your Watershed Moment

Story (Personal story: major life changes): Sitting in the tiny space my daughter called a 'cupboard', waiting for the sale of my home to go through and the funds to be released, I saw in a flash that my life would need to change even more radically. In moving towards unfolding the meaning in my own life, I would need to move away from where I now lived and cross the country to make a new life in another place, in another city, in another climate. In this watershed moment, I realised that I would like to work with folks who have experienced trauma and who are struggling to make their now changed lives meaningful. For this reason, I applied to several universities to do a PhD. One accepted me, and I embarked upon a cross-country journey to unfold my meaning out of difficulties and challenges, by working towards helping others to unfold and find theirs. In all of this, I forgot about my own sorrow and heartbreak, while simultaneously creating joy in other people's lives.

Story Essence: It's important to see life's difficulties and tragedies as potential watershed moments, so that we can fundamentally change the way we react to these circumstances. We can think of these challenges as calling us to be the best that we can be, to rise out of these moments and reach for something greater than ourselves.

Specific Action: If this were your watershed moment, think about what you can do to reach for something greater than yourself. Turn this moment into something wonderful for someone, somewhere. Write down your ideas.

In seeing our difficulties as potential watershed moments of change and rising up to be the best that we can be in those moments, we overcome and transform these tragedies. Tomorrow we will look at finding your personal

calling.

Day 13 – My Notes

§

Day 14 – We are Whole as We Are. We Are All Right

Story (Jack Kerouac): "I have lots of things to teach you now; in case we ever meet, concerning the message that was transmitted to me under a pine tree on a cold winter day. It said that in our true blissful essence of mind is known that everything is alright forever and forever and forever ... Close your eyes, let your hands and nerve-ends drop, stop breathing for 3 seconds, listen to the silence inside the illusion of the world." [6] These are the words of Jack Kerouac. If you were to think of your life as a story, a story with plots and sub-plots, one can think of life having a deeper plot, a kind of golden thread, which runs through our story, our reason for being here, an underlying deeper and more ultimate meaning. Without all the trappings of the

---

[6] Part of a letter to his wife Edie Kerouac Parker found in *The Portable Jack Kerouac.*

illusory world, in this silence when we stop the buzzing, when we are still, we are alright.

Story Essence: In our true and ultimate reality we have the potential to awaken to feel deeply that we are really alright. We can find our deeper meaning, our golden thread, without the noise and distractions of this world. We are whole as we are. We do not need to be anything else. We just need to be still in the chaos.

Specific Action: Simply be with yourself. Continue to breathe. Focus on this breath. Breathe in, breathe out, gently. Drop into this moment. Don't judge, just be still and keep coming back to your breath. Good job! Keep notes on how you feel after being in the moment and focusing on your breath. Contemplate what your personal calling or deeper plot might be. Write down your ideas.

In our true essence of mind, everything is all right; things are as they should be. In becoming awakened to the potential to find the deeper plot of our lives, we come to realise a personal calling, a deep meaning. In this way, our difficulties seem to simply be part of the journey. Tomorrow we will look at our calling as something that requires us to reach out.

Day 14 – My Notes

§

Day 15 – The Call that Beckons us to Find our Destiny

Story (James Hillman): According to James Hillman, one of the greatest mysteries of human nature is the question of character and destiny. In his bestseller *The Soul's Code*, he proposed that our calling in life is inborn and that it's our mission in life to realise its imperatives. He called it the 'acorn theory' – the idea that our lives are formed by a particular image, just as the oak's destiny is contained in the tiny acorn. Hillman says: *"It's Plato's myth that you come into the world with a destiny. The acorn theory says that there is an individual image that belongs to your soul ... your heart holds the image of your destiny and calls you to it."*[7]

---

[7] Interview on Scott London's website:
http://www.scottlondon.com/interviews/hillman.html

Story Essence: What is the destiny that you hold in your heart? What is the image that will become your calling, the reason for which you were born? Hillman calls on us to listen to this to find this image that belongs to our soul.

Specific Action: Think about the projects you've been involved in recently. What are the things that make you feel absorbed? What makes you feel happy when you're doing it? What are the things that you value? Ask others about a time that they thought you were at your best. What were you working on? Who were you working with? Keep a journal on what comes out of this search for the next week. This process will help to give you some clarity on what your calling might be.

By listening to the call of our destiny and finding the individual image of this destiny in our hearts, we lessen our struggles and we see more clearly what we need to do to align with our own unique calling. We will look tomorrow

at our unique life space.

Day 15 – My Notes

§

Day 16 – Filling Our Unique Life Space

Story (Helen Martins): Helen Martins was an outsider artist, someone who has had no training in the arts and lived in a small dry Karoo town, in the heart of the arid region of South Africa. Her life was stuck in darkness and, as the youngest of ten children, she was neglected by her father and a mother who became confined to bed. She was deeply shy and felt plain and unattractive. Her father was a large figure who abused his wife. Once her parents had passed away, she woke one night from a dream. In this dream she saw light, light out of the darkness of her life. She began to let light into her home by crushing up many colours of glass, fixing it to her walls, creating glass suns on the windows and hanging mirrors everywhere to reflect the light. She loved owls and created them almost wherever your eyes fell, with large glass eyes. In this way she transformed her life which had been one of sad darkness, to one of light, in her Owl House.

Story Essence: Despite her awful suffering and darkness, Helen Martins literally rose up out of the dark and ashes of her life. Her home today is a museum, visited by people from all over the world. In a very real way, she filled her special place, which only she could fill. As her vision began to grow, so her outer world began to glow.

Specific Action: How do you think you can fill your unique space? How will this uniqueness inside of you begin to glow? Think of how something in your life might begin to unfold. What is this *'something'*?

By finding our unique space, we can literally emerge out of darkness and suffering. Instead of feeling sad, we begin to feel a unique purpose. Tomorrow we will consider

again our freedom to choose, the freedom of our will.

Day 16 – My Notes

§

Day 17 – What is Your Choice of Response?

Story (The Buddha): A surly young man one day shouted at the Buddha, *"Go away! You just want to take advantage of us! You teachers come here to say a few pretty words and then ask for food and money!"*[8] But the Buddha was unruffled by these insults. He remained calm, exuding a feeling of loving-kindness. He politely requested that the man come forward. Then he asked, *"Young sir, if you purchased a lovely gift for someone, but that person did not accept the gift, to whom does the gift then belong?"* The odd question took the young man by surprise. *"I guess the gift would still be mine because I was the one who bought it".* *"Exactly so,"* replied the Buddha. *"Now, you have just cursed me and been angry with me. But if I do not*

---

[8] From: *The Very Delicious Strawberry*, Twenty illustrated Zen stories adapted for children, by Tim Johnson and Andrea Brajnovic.

accept your curses, if I do not get insulted and angry in return, these curses will fall back upon you—the same as the gift returning to its owner."

Story Essence: Once we understand that we have the free will to choose how we respond to any given situation, we can choose not to move to anger, just as the Buddha did when he did not accept the young man's curses. By pausing for a moment, you can become more mindful and more skilful in dealing with your thoughts and emotions.

Specific Action: The next time you feel angry, step back for a moment and pause. Just for this small moment, you can choose not to respond in anger. Write down each time you manage to do this.

In choosing not to move to anger, we become more resilient and skilful in our interactions with others, while also minimising our own suffering and the suffering of those around us. Tomorrow we will revisit something to

live for.

Day 17 – My Notes

§

Day 18 – Finding Something to Live For

Story (Temple Grandin): Temple Grandin appeared in the Time 100 List of the most influential people in the world, in the 'Heroes' category. Temple was born autistic. She created a 'hug box' to help her cope with her fear and anxiety. Whenever she felt scared, Temple would go on all fours inside her box. She would crawl into this strange-looking machine, pull a lever and the padded wooden walls would close in on her to give her a hug whenever she needed it. Her head would stick out as the hug box put pressure on her body. Once inside, she would sigh with relief. Her anxiety and fear would subside.

From an early age she connected closely with animals, especially cattle. Because she felt so threatened by her surroundings, she could understand how animals felt. Her condition and her connection with animals led to her discovering her calling. Today she is a spokesperson for humane animal handling methods. She is adamant that animals are not things and has designed many humane slaughterhouses in America. Today she is a doctor of animal science and a Professor at Colorado State University. Temple found her why. According to Friedrich Nietzsche: *"He who has a why to live for can bear almost any how."*

Story Essence: Temple had severe struggles with autism. Not only did she work to overcome these struggles, she also dealt with discrimination in the male-dominated field of animal husbandry as she built her career. How was she able to do this? Because she found her 'why': she found her something to live for, so as long as she remained focused on fulfilling her mission, nothing else mattered. No struggle could shift her focus from her reason for living.

Today she truly is a hero, an advocate for autism, for women, for animals.

Specific Action: For a moment become still, focus on your breathing, each time you have thoughts or distracting feelings, just gently come back to your breath, do not judge, drop into the moment. Try to do this for 5 to 10 minutes. When you have finished, think about your own why. Start with the things in your life that are worth living for. When you find what it is that you're here to offer the world, everything else will seem inconsequential compared to your reason for being alive. Write down the things you feel you can offer.

In finding our own special something to live for, our very own why, we can find our way more easily through the storms of life. This why fortifies us, gives us strength to overcome. Tomorrow we will revisit life questions.

Day 18 – My Notes

84

§

Day 19 – Life Questions and Light in the Darkness

Story (Viktor Frankl, Man's Search for Meaning): "I was struggling to find the reason for my sufferings, my slow dying". Viktor Frankl was emaciated and covered in nothing but rags. He knew he was dying; he was grey like the sky, flat and thin like paper. *"In a last violent protest against the hopelessness of imminent death, I sensed my spirit piercing through the enveloping gloom. I felt it transcend that hopeless, meaningless world, and from somewhere I heard a victorious 'Yes' in answer to my question of the existence of an ultimate purpose. At that moment a light was lit in a distant farmhouse, which stood on the horizon as if painted there, in the midst of the miserable grey of a dawning morning in Bavaria ... and the light shineth in the darkness."* The world and our lives are not purposeless. No matter what our circumstances, no matter how awful or difficult, there is always light to be found somewhere in the darkness.

Story Essence: Viktor Frankl got his answer to the question: is there meaning, is there ultimate purpose? When life questions you in difficult times, you can find ways to create meaning through and from these difficulties. Life is always filled with meaning and YES, it is always meaningful, no matter what, or how awful our circumstances may be!

Specific Action: Think for a moment about the meaning within your difficulty. It's tempting to assume that there's no meaning, but that's only if you have that assumption to begin with, then everything will support that assumption. Take the assumption that the meaning IS there, you just have to find it. Then you too can answer, "YES, it is there".

How do you think you will find it? Write this down as a reminder to yourself.

When the difficulties of life question us about the meaning of these challenges, we can face them with courage by saying: "Yes, there is meaning in these challenges, they are not purposeless". Tomorrow we will revisit the power of love.

Day 19 – My Notes

§

Day 20 – The Experience of Love; "The Salvation of Man"

Story (Viktor Frankl, Man's Search for Meaning): While hacking at the icy ground, Frankl was thinking about his wife and the love that he felt for her. Even though she was not present and Viktor did not even know if she was still alive, his love for her sustained him. He says *"The guard passed by, insulting me, and once again I communed with my beloved. More and more I felt that she was present, that she was with me; I had the feeling that I was able to touch her, able to stretch out my hand and grasp hers. The feeling was very strong: she was there. Then, at that very moment, a bird flew down silently and perched just in front of me, on the heap of soil which I had dug up from the ditch, and looked steadily at me."*

Story Essence: In unspoken ways love reaches us, whether the person we love is present, alive or not. This is the power of love to sustain us in life. For Viktor Frankl, *"the salvation of man is in love and through love."*

Specific Action: Who do you love? It could be a person with you, a person lost. It could be a friend, a child, a partner, a parent, a relative. It could even be a companion pet that you love, that gives meaning to your life. Think about this, create a feeling of really valuing this love and being grateful for it. Picture how they would want you to triumph over your difficulty and picture how much they would enjoy a version of you that has triumphed in this way. Smile: love has just come to your rescue.

The power of love to sustain us through all our storms and difficulties is really profound. In loving, feeling loved or remembering love, we are sustained no matter what our circumstances. Remember that love is immutable and eternal and can never be done away with. Tomorrow we

will consider self-compassion.

Day 20 – My Notes

§

Day 21 – Are You Your Own Best Friend?

Story (Tara Brach and Carl Rogers): "When I was in college, I went off to the mountains for a weekend of hiking with an older, wiser friend. After we set up our tent, we sat by a stream, watching the water swirl around rocks and talking about our lives. At one point she described how she was learning to be 'her own best friend'. A huge wave of sadness came over me, and I broke down sobbing. I was the farthest thing from my own best friend. I was continually harassed by an inner judge who was merciless, relentless, nit-picking, driving, often invisible but always on the job." [9]

This is Tara Brach's story.

---

[9] Tara Brach, "The Power of Radical Acceptance: Healing Trauma through the Integration of Buddhist Meditation and Psychotherapy".

Story Essence: Through the realisation of her profound sadness at not being kind to herself, Tara Brach developed the idea of radical self-acceptance. By accepting how you are feeling in the present moment, being with it and regarding it with compassion, we can transform these moments to enable us to reach towards the future, to go forward, to become unstuck. Carl Rogers wrote: *"The curious paradox is that when I accept myself just as I am, then I can change."* [10]

Specific Action: Each time you find yourself being unkind or critical about yourself, catch yourself. Stop yourself in that moment. Accept how you are feeling. Be kind to yourself. Say to yourself: "Isn't that interesting!" Then let it go. Think of something you have felt that was positive, and let this new feeling fill you. Savour that feeling for a moment.

---

[10] Carl R. Rogers, *On Becoming a Person: A Therapist's View of Psychotherapy.*

Self-acceptance and self-kindness enable us to change. In this way we can grow out of our suffering and self-inflicted negativity. Tomorrow we will consider our attitudes in times of difficulty.

Day 21 – My Notes

§

Day 22 – Is It Ever OK to Give Up Hope?

Story: (Viktor Frankl, Man's Search for Meaning): *"Unless there was 100% guarantee that I will be killed here on the spot, and I will never survive this concentration camp ... unless there is any guarantee, I'm responsible for living from now on in a way that I may make use of the slightest chance of survival, ignoring the great danger surrounding me."* This is how Viktor Frankl was able to learn to cope during his time in a concentration camp in Nazi Germany. It somehow gave him hope.

Story Essence: By thinking that there was no guarantee that he would not survive, Viktor Frankl found a way to keep hoping and thinking that there was a chance he could come out of this terrible situation in the horrific conditions in which he found himself. In the same way, we, too, can change our own attitudes in times of difficulty.

Specific Action: Think about your own ways of coping with difficult situations. The next time you feel that there's no hope left, and that everything is going to hell, ask yourself, "Am I absolutely guaranteed to be destroyed by this situation? Is there any chance at all that I might still make it through this alive?" If there is, take heart. That is your light. This makes you stronger. Know that in that moment, it's time to simply accept the looming problem that seems so troubling.

When we think that there is a chance that things will be different, that things will pass and will change, it gives us hope. This helps us to cope and not feel overcome by feelings of despair. Tomorrow we will think about challenges and how you overcome them.

Day 22 – My Notes

99

§

Day 23 – Going With the Flow

Story (Taoist story): A Taoist story tells of an old man who accidentally fell into the river rapids leading to a high and dangerous waterfall. Onlookers feared for his life. Miraculously, he came out alive and unharmed downstream at the bottom of the falls. People asked him how he managed to survive: *"I accommodated myself to the water, not the water to me. Without thinking, I allowed myself to be shaped by it. Plunging into the swirl, I came out with the swirl. This is how I survived."* [11]

Story Essence: Like the man in this story, you too can work with what life gives you. Accept difficulties as part of life. Know that you are developing a deep inner strength to deal with all of life's challenges, joys and unfolding.

---

[11] Unknown origin; quoted on https://taoist-arts.com/News_-Views/Chinese_Philosophy_/Zen_and_Taoist_Stories/zen_and_taoist_stories.html

Specific Action: The next time you feel that wave of turbulence coming over you, feel yourself plunging into it like the man in this story. Instead of falling apart, lean into the turbulence. Know that it is only by accepting it that you triumph over it.

Accepting a situation, going with it, helps us to come through it, even if it is difficult. By going with the flow of life, we become resilient, bending but not breaking. Tomorrow we will think about courage.

Day 23 – My Notes

§

Day 24 – Good News! You do not Have the Heart of a Mouse

Story (Indian fable): According to an ancient Indian fable, a mouse was in constant distress because of its fear of the cat. A magician took pity on it and turned it into a cat. But then it became afraid of the dog. So the magician turned it into a dog. Then it began to fear the panther. So the magician turned it into a panther. Immediately it became full of fear for the hunter. At this point the magician gave up, and turned it into a mouse again saying, *"Nothing I do for you is going to be of any help because you have the heart of a mouse".* [12]

Story Essence: As you begin to near the end of your daily stories, lessons and actions to take, I know that you will not have the 'heart of a mouse'. I know that the

---

[12] Unknown. Source: *101 Zen Stories*.

strength that you are building will motivate and inspire you not to give in to fearfulness.

Specific Action: Think about a time you have been courageous. Keep this feeling with you. Take it into yourself, allow it to deepen. Say to yourself, "I have courage, I am strong, and I am going forward".

Having 'the heart of a mouse' keeps us in a fearful state. Being in this state causes us to suffer. By having courage, we can weather the storms of life. Tomorrow we revisit your personal calling.

Day 24 – My Notes

§

Day 25 – It is Time for Self-Transcendence

Story (Henry Ford; Thomas Edison; Beethoven and Albert Einstein): Henry Ford failed in business several times and went bankrupt five times before he founded the Ford Motor Company. Thomas Edison as a young man was told by his teachers that he was "too stupid to learn anything". Beethoven was so awkward on the violin that his teachers believed him hopeless as a composer. Albert Einstein originally started out as a patent clerk.

Story Essence: These stories illustrate the power of transformation. As Viktor Frankl said, the human being is capable of self-transcendence. We are capable of reaching great heights out of mediocrity. We are deeply spiritual beings. In the words of Jack Kerouac: *"You will remember the lesson you forgot, it is all one vast awakened thing. I call it the golden eternity".*

Specific Action: Think now of one thing that you can do to rise out of the ordinary. Then do it. Feel the sense of excitement that you have: it is this excitement that will propel you forward, to the task that only you can do.

By thinking about and taking action in the things that only we can do, we are capable of self-transcendence, of transforming our lives out of troubles and into joys. Tomorrow we look at igniting humour in our lives.

Day 25 – My Notes

§

Day 26 – Igniting Humour

Story (Viktor Frankl, Man's Search for Meaning): A prisoner accidentally bumps into a Nazi guard. The guard turns and shouts, *"Schwein!"* (This means 'pig' in German). The prisoner bows and says, *"Cohen. Pleased to meet you"*. The joke clearly demonstrates how humour helps to reverse who's in control and who seems to be the superior being. Even in the terrible conditions of the Nazi concentration camp, such jokes provided a means of momentarily overcoming extreme adversity.

Story Essence: In our circumstances of adversity, we need to try to remember that humour can lift us out of our situation. Frankl said: *"I would never have made it if I could not have laughed. Laughing lifted me momentarily out of this horrible situation, just enough to make it liveable ... survivable"*. If you ever see His Holiness the

Dalai Lama, you will notice that he is often laughing. This gives him a child-like quality that is irresistible. He knows the tragedies of this time, yet is also able to find moments of joy and light-heartedness. Maybe we can find ways to take ourselves less seriously?

Specific Action: Think now about how you might be able to find humour in a difficult situation. I often think that these situations are sent to humble us. Finding that humour in your situation will no doubt make it more liveable. Humour is always lurking in every situation: you just have to find it. When you do, smile: you are doing well.

In finding humour in our situation, no matter how difficult, we can create lightness about it, rather than heaviness. Tomorrow we will consider a power that is uniquely human.

Day 26 – My Notes

§

Day 27 – Accessing a Power that is Uniquely Human

Story (T. Shantall on Viktor Frankl): In the words of Viktor Frankl *"For what ... counts and matters is to bear witness to the uniquely human potential at its best, which is to transform a tragedy into a personal triumph, to turn one's predicament into a human achievement".* Imagine for example, in the case of an incurable disease: when we cannot change a situation, we are challenged to change ourselves. Even if we can no longer change our fate, Frankl says that *"by rising above and growing beyond ourselves, we exercise the most creative of human potentials".*[13]

Story Essence: When we can't change a situation that is beyond our control, we are challenged to change our attitude and to change ourselves. Simply by accepting your

---

[13] T. Shantall, *The Quest for Destiny.*

circumstances you can make deep changes to your life. Recognise today that this is one of our most impressive abilities as human beings. It is in essence the miracle of our existence.

Specific Action: Choose one situation today that you can change your attitude towards. What will you change? In what ways will you change yourself? You, too, can begin to harness the greatest of your human abilities, the ability to rise above your situation.

By recognising our ability to change ourselves in situations that are beyond our control, we become exponentially more powerful, able to bear our difficulties, able to triumph. Tomorrow we look at relieving our loved ones of suffering.

Day 27 – My Notes

§

Day 28 – Relieve your Loved Ones from Suffering

Story (Viktor Frankl, Man's Search for Meaning): An elderly, depressed patient who could not get over the loss of his wife was helped by the following conversation with Frankl. Frankl asked: *"What would have happened if you had died first, and your wife would have had to survive you?"* *"Oh,"* replied the patient, *"for her this would have been terrible; how she would have suffered!"* Frankl continued: *"You see such a suffering has been spared her; and it is you who have spared her this suffering; but now, you have to pay for it by surviving her and mourning her."* The man said no word, but shook Frankl's hand and calmly left his office.

Story Essence: Through the power of love we can change our mind-set from one of despair. Instead we can see ourselves sparing those we love from unhappiness. In thinking how his wife would suffer at his loss, he was able to change his own attitude towards his feeling of loss.

Specific Action: Think of a situation in your life where you can help someone you love by changing your attitude towards your own suffering or loss? Your suffering doesn't only hurt you, it also hurts the ones you love, sometimes even more deeply than it hurts you. By recognising this, you can find strength knowing that you are relieving their suffering when you find ways to relieve your own suffering. What action can you take today to change your attitude towards your suffering and spare those you love or care about from suffering?

By changing our attitude to suffering, keeping in mind our loved ones and sparing them from unhappiness at our suffering, we can triumph even in this situation.

Day 28 – My Notes

§

Day 29 – Doing the One Thing that I Know is Right

Story (Southwick et al.): In an article about the use of a meaning-based intervention (Logotherapy) to treat chronic combat-related PTSD, the authors offer a case study of a post-traumatic stress disorder sufferer who had a sense of doom, of no future. As a result of getting help with finding meaning and reaching out and helping others, he said: *"I never thought I'd look in the mirror and see a 52 year old staring back. Never dreamed I'd live this long and I feel like I've wasted a lot of time just waiting for the ax to fall. I think now that if I continue to practice doing that one thing every day that I know in my heart is right, maybe my life will have meant something. Those kids I tutor have taught me a lot about my own family and myself. They know when I'm supposed to arrive and they can't wait to see me and now I've got that with my grandkids. What's most important for me now is to be there for them, not let them down."[14]*

Story Essence: Someone who has experienced a traumatic event like war, criminal violence, or a car accident for example, could suffer from PTSD, which can become a chronic psychological problem, severely affecting the life of the person. For this particular PTSD sufferer, doing the one thing that he felt in his heart was right meant reaching out to tutor disadvantaged kids. In this way, he felt that his life had a purpose after all.

Specific Action: Think the following: "May I be filled with loving-kindness. May I be safe from inner and outer dangers. May I be well in body and mind. May I be at ease and happy." Then extend this out to those you love. Extend

---

[14] Southwick et al., "Logotherapy as an Adjunctive Treatment for Chronic Combat-related PTSD: A Meaning-based Intervention".

this now to your community. From here send it out to the country, to the world and to all beings who may be suffering. Good job. How can you reach out to and help others? What one thing can you do that you know is right?

By never giving up, by constantly reaching out to and sending love to others, we lift ourselves out of our own difficulties. Create the habit of doing this daily. Every time you do it, it becomes a stronger part of who you are, and makes the world a more joyful place as a direct result of you being in it.

Day 29 – My Notes

121

§

Day 30 – I Broke my Neck: it Didn't Break Me

Story (Jerry Long): In *Logotherapy for Clinical Practice* the story of Jerry Long is told. Jerry *"was a teenage baseball player whose pitching had the attention of the professional leagues. Then he broke his neck and became physically dependent on others for his most basic activities of daily living. While he recognised that his potential for an athletic career had vanished, he also came to realise that much freedom remained in other areas in which he could actualise personal life meaning. He took responsibility for implementing that freedom: graduated from high school, went on to college, and eventually earned his doctorate in clinical psychology and became a practicing logotherapist. He was able to lead a fulfilling life in spite of being a quadriplegic. He often summed up succinctly his inspiring credo for life: 'I broke my neck; it didn't break me.' He took responsibility to do what he could, within the freedom that he had, to establish and maintain an attitude to pursue a personal life meaning, in spite of his physical condition.* "[15]

Story Essence: Don't let your own situation break you. Discover where your freedoms are, and explore how you can use those freedoms to continue finding a reason to live. Like Jerry Long, you, too, are free to make the choice to exercise this freedom of choice, to choose a project, or to give back to others in a loving way or bear your unavoidable suffering with dignity. In this way, your suffering becomes a triumph.

Specific Action: By finding your meaning and purpose you will come to know success and happiness. Think about a cause you can get involved in today, then go out there and

---

[15] Schulenberg et al., "Logotherapy for Clinical Practice".

give your time to this cause. Like Jerry Long, you must not allow your situation to break you, no matter how dire it seems.

Day 30 – My Notes

§

Final Message

Through finding ways to unfold your meaning, you have been on a journey to overcome life's difficulties. In the process you have become more skilful in your interactions, more mindful of your life, more kind to yourself and others, and more accepting of the multiple ways in which life can unfold. I wish you well for your future: may you go forward with lightness, kindness, purpose, meaning and humour.

My New Blueprint for Living

127

My changed attitudes and how I have turned difficulties into triumphs:

"Everything can be taken from a man but one thing: the last of the human freedoms – to choose one's attitude in any given set of circumstances, to choose one's own way." (Frankl, 2006)

Ways in which I am or will be using my gifts or actualising my personal calling:

Ways in which I have improved or enhanced my relationships or found new beauty or love in my life:

Ways in which I have accepted things I cannot change. Ways in which I will bear my suffering with dignity:

*"When we are no longer able to **change** a situation, we are challenged to **change** ourselves."* (Frankl, 2006)

Ways in which my suffering or difficulties have made me stronger:

"Suffering is intended to guard us from our apathy, from psychic rigor mortis. In fact, we mature in suffering, grow because of it – it makes us richer and stronger." (Frankl, 2006)

My personal calling is:

These are the ways that I will practice self-compassion:

These are the ways that I will become more mindful of my responses and my actions:

References

101 Zen Stories. Retrieved from:
http://www.venerabilisopus.org/en/

Brach, T. "The Power of Radical Acceptance: Healing Trauma through the Integration of Buddhist Meditation and Psychotherapy". Retrieved from:
https://www.tarabrach.com/articles-interviews/trauma/

Frankl, V. E. (2006). *Man's Search for Meaning*. Boston: Beacon Press.

Grand, R; Grillo, M; Nanas, H, (Producers), & Brooks, A., (Director). (1991). *Defending Your Life* [Motion Picture]. United States: Warner Bros.

Hillman, J. (2017). *The Soul's Code: In Search of Character and Calling*. USA: Ballantine Books; Reprint edition.

Johnson, T. (Author), & Brajnovic, A. (Illustrator). (2015). *The Very Delicious Strawberry: Twenty Illustrated Zen Stories Adapted for Children*. USA: Amazon Digital Services.

Keller, H. (1918) "What is the IWW?": Speech given at the New York City Civic Club, January 1918), quoted in Helen Keller: Her Socialist Years (International Publishers, 1967).

Kerouac. J. (1996). *The Portable Jack Kerouac*. New York: Penguin Books; Reprint edition.

London, S. (2012). "On Soul, Character and Calling: A Conversation with James Hillman". Retrieved from: http://www.scottlondon.com/interviews/hillman.html

Rogers, C. (1995). *On Becoming a Person: A Therapist's View of Psychotherapy.* New York: Houghton Mifflin 2nd edition.

Schulenberg, S. E., Hutzell, R. R., Nassif, C., Rogina, J. M. (2008). "Logotherapy for Clinical Practice". *Psychotherapy: Theory, Research, Practice, Training, 45*(4): 447-463.

Shantall, T. (2004). *The Quest for Destiny: A Logotherapeutic Guide to Meaning-centred Living, Therapy and Counselling.* Pretoria: Unisa Press.

Southwick, S., Gilmartin, R., McDonough, P., & Morrissey, P. (2006). "Logotherapy as an Adjunctive Treatment for Chronic Combat-related PTSD: A Meaning-based Intervention". *American Journal of Psychotherapy. 60(2):*161-74.

Appendix

The conceptual framework of this workbook is based on the thoughts of Viktor Frankl in *Man's Search for Meaning* and *Logotherapy*.

Concept 1 – **Freedom of the Will** – This relates to our power of choice. We are free to choose our attitudes. According to Viktor Frankl:

"Everything can be taken from a man but one thing: the last of the human freedoms – to choose one's attitude in any given set of circumstances, to choose one's own way." (Frankl, 2006)

Concept 2 – **Will to Meaning** – According to Frankl, this relates to one's desire to find and create meaning in one's life:

"Striving to find meaning in one's life is the primary motivational force in man." (Frankl, 2006)

Concept 3 – **Meaning in Life** – In the thought of Viktor Frankl, it is clear that meaning in life can be found in any moment of living, even during periods of difficulty and suffering, and, even at the moment of death until the last breath.

i)   **Creative values** – creative actions that you can take. This involves making use of our gifts or personal calling by reaching out to others and contributing to society.

ii)   **Experiential values** – this links to relationships and relating to people. We can find meaning through beauty, truth and love.

iii)   **Attitudinal values** – This links to finding meaning in suffering. We can change our attitude to suffering by viewing it in a positive way. In Frankl's words:

*"When we are no longer able to **change** a situation, we are challenged to **change** ourselves."* (Frankl, 2006).

Concept 4 – **The Meaning of Suffering** – We have a choice to think of the suffering we experience in life as a challenge. As Frankl says:

"Suffering is intended to guard us from our apathy, from psychic rigor mortis. In fact, we mature in suffering, grow because of it – it makes us richer and stronger." (Frankl, 2006)

Concept 5 – **Personal Destiny – Is Meaning a Personal Calling?** There is a body of research that demonstrates that a person experiences life as meaningful, when serving or reaching towards something greater than themselves, such as a greater good. This could be thought of as a personal calling. According to Teria Shantall in the book, *The Quest for Destiny*:

"A life-task or destiny is given, something assigned to us..." (Shantall, 2004).

www.ingramcontent.com/pod-product-compliance
Lightning Source LLC
Chambersburg PA
CBHW031339060726
47590CB00007B/2546